3006 2656

12/03

W9-BLD-247

GYMNASTICS
FOR FUN!

By Beth Gruber

Content Adviser: Glenn Aser, Gymnastics Coach, New York, New York
Reading Adviser: Frances J. Bonacci, Reading Specialist, Cambridge, Massachusetts

COMPASS POINT BOOKS
MINNEAPOLIS, MINNESOTA

Compass Point Books
3109 West 50th Street, #115
Minneapolis, MN 55410

Visit Compass Point Books on the Internet at *www.compasspointbooks.com*
or e-mail your request to *custserv@compasspointbooks.com*

Photographs ©: Jim Cummins/Getty Images, front cover (left), Comstock, front cover (right),
back cover; Mike Powell/Getty Images, 4–5, 20–21; Jamie Squire/Getty Images, 7; Gary M. Prior/
Getty Images, 8–9; Getty Royalty Free, 10, 42 (top right), 45 (bottom left); Courtesy of Deary's
Gymnastics Supply, 11; Doug Pensinger/Getty Images, 13, 24–25, 29, 31, 34–35, 38–39; Adam Pretty/
Getty Images, 14–15; Corel, 17, 19 (left), 33, 44, 47; Getty Images, 19, (right), 43; Mike Hewitt/
Getty Images, 23; Phil Cole/Getty Images, 26–27; Billy Stickland/Getty Images, 36–37; Ken Levine/
Getty Images, 40–41; Tony Duffy/Getty Images, 41, 42 (bottom right); Steve Powell/Getty Images, 45
(center top); Mark Mainz/ Getty Images, 45.

Editor: Elizabeth Bond/Bill SMITH STUDIO
Photo Researchers: Sandra Will, Sean Livingstone, and Christie Silver/Bill SMITH STUDIO
Designer: Colleen Sweet/Bill SMITH STUDIO

Library of Congress Cataloging-in-Publication Data
   Gruber, Beth.
   Gymnastics for fun! / by Beth Gruber.
   p. cm. — (Sports for fun!)
   Summary: Describes the sport of gymnastics and presents information on the basic equipment,
   practice, coaching, and competition.
   Includes bibliographical references and index.
   ISBN 0-7565-0487-2 (hardcover : alk. paper)
   1. Gymnastics—Juvenile literature. [1. Gymnastics.] I. Title. II.
   Series.
   GV461.3.G78 2003
   796.44—dc21
                        2003006673

Table of Contents

Ground Rules

The Main Event

People, Places, and Fun

Note: In this book, there are two kinds of vocabulary words. Gymnastics Words to Know are words specific to gymnastics. They are in **bold** and are defined on page 46. Other Words to Know are helpful words that aren't related only to gymnastics. They are in ***bold and italicized.*** These are defined on page 47.

Let's Get Rolling!

Every four years, fans of all ages tune their TV sets to the Olympics to watch the gymnastics events. What makes this sport so exciting? Gymnasts make beautiful shapes with their bodies. They perform daredevil feats at amazing heights and speeds. Gymnasts are strong and have incredible athletic ability. They must be *flexible* and *agile.* Gymnasts perform astonishing moves on the floor, on the bars, on the beam, and even in midair.

Some gymnastics events are performed by both girls and boys. However, because they have different levels of strength in different parts of their bodies, some events are only performed by boys while others are done only by girls.

It takes years of training to be a great gymnast. So how does a gymnast get started? Let's get rolling and find out!

Apparatus	Who Does What?
Balance Beam	Girls Only
Uneven Bars	Girls Only
Pommel Horse	Boys Only
Rings	Boys Only
Parallel Bars	Boys Only
Horizontal Bar	Boys Only
Vault	Girls & Boys
Floor Exercise	Girls & Boys

On the Floor

All gymnasts train in **gymnasiums,** or gyms for short. Gyms come in many shapes and sizes. Some gyms look like the *arenas* in which gymnasts compete. Some gyms have special areas for *spectators* to sit and watch practices or competitions. Most gyms have big holes in the floor called "pits." Pits are lined with foam and filled with foam blocks. Pits and **safety mats** provide *cushioned* areas for gymnasts to land when they perform a **dismount.**

Gymnasts compete on special equipment called **apparatus.** Most gyms have the same apparatuses that are used in Olympic events. For competition, the apparatuses for male and female events are arranged separately. If you look at the picture, you might recognize the **balance beam, parallel bars, vaulting horse, horizontal bar,** and a carpeted area of **floor** bordered by a white line. In gymnastics, even the floor is a piece of equipment!

balance beam

floor

vaulting horse

horizontal bar

parallel bars

What's Your Game?

There are two types of gymnastics that you will see at a gymnastics event. In **artistic gymnastics,** athletes perform on the apparatuses. Each apparatus is used for a specific event. Boys and girls compete in events that are best suited to their body types.

Another form of gymnastics is called **rhythmic gymnastics.** In this event, female gymnasts perform with an apparatus. Rhythmic gymnasts use balls, ropes, hoops, ribbons, or a set of clubs in their events. They can compete individually or in a group. In all events, the apparatus becomes an extension of the gymnast's body with every move she makes. **Routines** for this event are performed on a floor mat to music. Rhythmic gymnastics is a beautiful and graceful sport to watch. It became an official Olympic sport in 1984.

ndividual rhythmic gymnastic exercises last
o more than 90 seconds and feature one
pparatus. Group exercises may feature
everal different apparatuses and last
s long as two minutes.

Suiting Up

If you play baseball, you can always take your ball and glove home, but if you're a gymnast, you have to leave your equipment at the gym! Like most athletes, gymnasts wear special clothing to help them perform.

Leotards are one-piece suits made of stretchy fabric that hug the body and help gymnasts move freely. Girls wear one-piece leotards or stretchy tank tops with tight, short bicycle pants. Boys wear sleeveless leotards under shorts for practice. In competition, they wear shorts for floor exercises and vaulting. They wear long tights for work on other apparatuses.

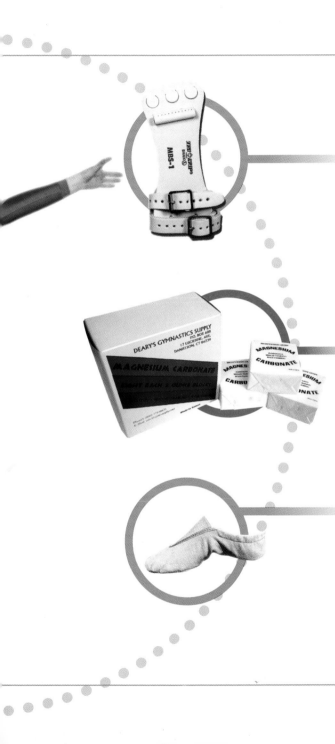

Hand guards, or grips, are leather straps that fit over the fingers and close at the wrist. They protect a gymnast's hands from skin tears and blisters. Gymnasts wear hand guards for work on the bars or the rings.

Powdered chalk helps gymnasts keep their hands and feet from getting sweaty. Gymnasts dip their hands and feet in chalk to keep from slipping.

Tumbling shoes are only used in floor exercise routines. They cover the foot and keep gymnasts from slipping.

Show Me How

Gymnasts train longer and harder than most other athletes. They often get tired and injured, so a good coach needs to know how to keep a gymnast healthy and motivated. Coaches help gymnasts stay on track when they would rather be out playing with friends. They push gymnasts to the next step in a difficult routine. When a gymnast gets injured, a coach knows just what to do to help the gymnast get back in the arena—maybe even in time for the next important competition. Coaches also know when to keep athletes from performing when they are injured, in order to prevent a more serious *injury.*

Coaches are a very important part of a gymnast's life. Each coach has a different personality and style of coaching, but all coaches are great teachers. The best coaches have one thing in common: They want to help a gymnast be the best he or she can be.

Everybody Knows His Name

Bela Karolyi was never much of a gymnast. The only time he tried the **pommel horse,** he broke his arm! But Bela is one of the best-known coaches in all of gymnastics. He has his own system for training, and he gets good results. He coached Olympic champions Nadia Comaneci and Mary Lou Retton. In the summer of 1996, he led America's "Magnificent Seven" (see p.39) to a women's Olympic team gold medal. Now that's a great coach!

Svetlana Boginskaia talks with her coach, Bela Karolyi.

Getting Started

Everyone learns to walk before learning to run. Gymnasts practice and learn to perform their amazing tricks exactly the same way. Four basic positions, used in all events, help them get started.

The Pike: Bend at your hip and keep your knees straight. Place your hands on the floor or behind your ankles. Gymnasts often use the pike position when dismounting from the balance beam.

The Tuck: Think about curling up like a ball. Pull your knees in close to your chest. Then, wrap both of your hands around your knees. The tuck is a good position to use when dismounting from a vaulting horse or table.

The Straddle: Spread your legs wide and raise your arms straight out to your sides. Keep your back straight and face forward. The straddle comes in handy in floor exercises and many other gymnastics routines.

The Layout: Stand on tiptoe and extend your arms upward. Hold your body in a straight line, from toes to fingertips. Every gymnastics routine ends with a layout. It is the most basic position of all.

Allana Slater of Australia uses the pike to dismount from the uneven bars.

Rolls, Handstands, and Cartwheels

Each gymnastics event requires different moves. These three basic moves are a great way to begin.

Rolls: Squat down and stretch your arms forward. Tuck your chin into your chest and use your legs to push off. Land on your palms and roll forward as you bring your legs over your body. Practice doing a forward roll. Then try one backward!

Handstands: Place a mat against a wall, then get down on the floor in a push-up position. Put your heels against the wall, and walk your feet up the wall as high as possible. Next, walk both hands back to the wall at the same time. Hold this position for a few seconds, then walk down the wall again. Repeating this exercise is a good way to get in shape to do handstands from a **freestanding** position.

Cartwheels: It is important to master the handstand before stepping up to this basic move. Begin with one foot in front of the other and stretch your arms upward. Next, kick over through the handstand position and follow through to the landing. Finish with your front leg slightly bent and keep your back leg straight.

Safety is important when performing freestanding moves like the handstand and cartwheel. Always ask an adult to stand by as your spotter to catch you if you slip and help prevent injury.

Walking the Tightrope

The balance beam is a piece of suede-covered wood with springy padding underneath. It is 16 feet (5 meters) long and 4 inches (10 centimeters) wide. Balance beam routines last between 70 and 90 seconds. Two **flight elements** must be included in the routine. A flight element is a series of moves performed in the air. A gymnast must use the entire length of the beam in a routine, and most often gymnasts go up and down the beam many times.

Balance beam and floor routines look a lot alike, but there is one big difference. It takes perfect *balance* to perform a somersault, split, cartwheel, or back flip on a narrow platform that's almost 4 feet (1.2 m) above the ground! No wonder gymnasts compare performing on a balance beam to walking on a tightrope!

The Munchkin of Munich

In 1972, Olga Korbut wowed the world when she "aced" the first back flip ever performed on a balance beam. Today, every gymnast does them. Her height of less than 5 feet (1.5 m) earned her the nickname "munchkin."

Flying High

The uneven bars are made of wood-covered *fiberglass.* In this event, gymnasts move between two bars: the high bar and the low bar. The high bar stands 7 feet (2 m) above the ground, and the low bar is only 5 feet (1.5 m) high. A distance of 5 to 6 feet (1.5 to 1.8 m) separates the bars.

A typical routine only lasts about 30 seconds, but each second of the routine is action-packed. In competition, the gymnast must perform at least two flight elements, change grips, and change directions. Gymnasts can only make five moves on one bar before they must move to the other bar.

The first gymnasts to perform on the uneven bars did a lot of balletlike moves. Today, gymnasts do swings, circles, handstands, twists, somersaults, and release moves.

Dominique Moceanu of the U.S. performs a release move during her routine at the 1996 Summer Olympic Games in Atlanta, Georgia.

Hands On

Male gymnasts compete on the pommel horse. The apparatus name comes from its appearance, because it used to have a head and tail like a horse. Standard routines last between 30 and 40 seconds. You might see a gymnast swing both legs together in circles around the horse. This is called a "double-leg circle." Gymnasts might also open their legs wide and swing them back and forth across the horse like a *pendulum.* This move is called the "scissors."

You won't see spectacular speed or tricks on the pommel horse. But that doesn't mean it is an easy event. It takes tremendous *strength* in the shoulders, arms, and wrists to perform on the pommel horse. And remember, the only part of a gymnast's body that can touch the horse is the hands!

The pommel horse is a padded suede or leather bench that sits on sturdy legs. It has two adjustable U-shaped handles called "pommels" on the top. The pommel horse measures 5 feet (1.5 m) long and is about 3 feet (1 m) high.

Kanukai Jackson of England performs on the pommel horse at the 2002 Commonwealth Games.

2002
Manchester
THE XVII COMMONWEALTH GAMES

Power Up

The **rings** take amazing strength, discipline, and patience. Most routines last between 30 and 50 seconds. During a typical routine, male gymnasts swing into a series of strength positions and do at least two handstands.

Familiar strength positions include the **L-support** and the **planche.** In the L-support, gymnasts keep their arms straight down and their *torsos* upright. Then they lift their legs straight out in front, to form an "L" with their legs and bodies. In the planche position, the gymnast's body is face down and parallel to the floor. His body must be above the rings. The most famous strength position is the **Iron Cross.** Even the best gymnasts can only hold this position for a few seconds!

Top scores are awarded to gymnasts who can keep the rings motionless and their bodies perfectly straight. Power and flexibility are the secrets to competing on this apparatus.

The rings are a pair of wooden or fiberglass hoops. Each ring is approximately 7 inches (18 cm) in diameter and hangs 8 feet (2.4 m) above the floor. Cables attach the rings to the top of a metal frame or to the ceiling.

Perfect Balance

It takes strong arm, chest, stomach, and leg muscles to excel on the parallel bars. Male gymnasts must also have good balance. Top performers will be able to keep their bodies straight, their arms locked, and their shoulders lined up above their hands.

Standard routines last between 25 and 30 seconds. Most gymnasts include big swings, somersaults, **aerial** somersaults called **saltos,** and stationary handstands in their routines. They soar above and below the bars or perform on just a single bar. Strength moves, like the L-support, are also used on the parallel bars. All parallel bars routines must include a release move. The gymnast lets go of the bar, performs a skill in midair, and catches the bar again.

The parallel bars are a pair of bouncy rods made of wood or wood-coated fiberglass. Each bar is 11 feet (3.4 m) long and stands 5 feet (1.5 m) above the floor. The distance between the two bars is a little more than the distance between a gymnast's shoulders.

Swing and Circle

The horizontal bar is sometimes called the high bar. Why? Because it is hung 8 feet (2.4 m) above the floor! It is so high, coaches must lift gymnasts up off the floor to help them get started. The horizontal bar is made of 1-inch-thick (2.5 cm) steel and is 7 feet (2 m) long. There are always mats below the horizontal bar to protect gymnasts from injury if they fall.

Most high bar routines last between 25 and 30 seconds. The routines include a lot of big forward and backward circles around the bar. In really exciting routines, male gymnasts will hold their bodies straight, bend their bodies, or even straddle the bar as they circle around it. All routines must include grip changes and catch-and-release moves. To keep from falling, gymnasts point their thumbs in the direction they are moving.

The horizontal bar is usually the last event at a competition. It is also the most exciting and the most dangerous. Crash landings are not fun when traveling upside-down through the air!

John Roethlisberger performs his horizontal bar routine at the 2000 U.S. Olympic Men's Gymnastic Trials.

Up and Over

Imagine traveling through the air at speeds greater than 17 miles (27 kilometers) per hour. Boys and girls perform difficult moves on the vault while soaring through the air at amazing speeds. Each vault routine has four steps: the **run-up, preflight, afterflight,** and the **landing.**

The run-up is the most important part of the vault. Gymnasts count the steps they take to make sure that they always land in the same place. At the very end of the run-up, the gymnast leaps onto a **springboard** in front of the vault and jumps up toward the horse. This is called preflight. In afterflight, gymnasts use their hands to push off the horse. Their goal is to get as high above the horse as possible. The higher the gymnast goes, the more tricks and moves he or she can do in the air before landing.

The vaulting horse is made of suede or leather and is padded underneath. It is 5 feet (1.5 m) long and 14 inches (36 cm) wide. The height can be adjusted between 4 feet (1.2 m) and 4 feet 5 inches (1.4 m). The vaulting horse looks like the pommel horse, but it doesn't have handles.

The final step of the vault is the landing. Gymnasts work hard to perfect their landings. They want to hit the mat with both feet and "stick" in that position. They try not to wobble or take extra steps because the judges will deduct points from their scores.

A typical vault only lasts about five seconds. But every second is thrilling!

ELITE™

AMERICAN

Fancy Feats

Girls and boys perform the floor exercise, but their routines include different types of elements.

Girls perform their routines to music. Their routines last from 70 to 90 seconds. Floor exercises for girls feature tumbling runs with handsprings, somersaults, back flips, and dance movements. Gymnasts pose and dance in and out of each corner as they tumble back and forth across the floor. They are judged on grace, balance, flexibility, and emotional expression.

Boys do not perform their routines to music or dance, and their routines are shorter. Boys' exercises are judged on strength, balance, and tumbling. They include some of the same moves used on the pommel horse, plus high-speed tumbling moves such as aerial somersaults. Like girls, boys must move across the entire floor. In the corners, they hold difficult poses like the **Y-scale.**

Floor exercises are performed on a carpeted area. The floor is 40 feet (12 m) long on each side and makes the shape of a square. The carpet sits on a platform that is soft and springy underneath. White lines mark the edges of the carpet. Beware! Gymasts are penalized for stepping outside the white lines while performing on the floor.

Shannon Miller strikes a pose during her floor routine exercise.

Practice Makes Perfect

You're right! It takes years of practice for gymnasts to learn all the incredible tricks they perform in competition.

First, gymnasts work on the basic moves and positions. It takes beginning gymnasts as long as one to two years to learn the basics. Once they have mastered the basics, gymnasts put different moves together to create a more difficult series of moves. These are called *progressions.* Long before they ever do a backward somersault on the balance beam, gymnasts practice them over and over on the floor. By the time a gymnast does a trick at a competition, he or she has practiced it thousands of times!

It's up to the coach to decide when a gymnast is ready to progress. Coaches design programs that help gymnasts build strong muscles. They check the gymnast's form. They also challenge the gymnast to get better every day. Coaches are trained to help gymnasts build skills safely and without injury. Safety is important when a gymnast is learning new skills!

Dominique Dawes of the U.S. performs on the balance
beam during the 1996 Summer Olympic Games.

At the Competitions

Gymnastics has two major competitions: the World Championships and the Summer Olympic Games. The World Championships are held every year, and the Summer Olympics take place every four years. In both of these competitions, the finest athletes from around the world come to compete.

Rules and regulations for gymnastics competitions are determined by the **Fédération Internationale de Gymnastique** (FIG). At a competition, six judges and a technical adviser watch each event and award each gymnast a score. Points are awarded based on the difficulty of the moves, *originality* and *composition,* and *execution.* A gymnast's total score is the average of all the judges' scores, except the highest and lowest scores.

For each routine, a gymnast begins with less than a perfect score of 10. Female gymnasts begin with a 9.00, and male gymnasts begin with an 8.60. Judges award points for extra tricks and subtract points for mistakes. A perfect score of 10 is very hard to achieve for a routine.

Judges watch and score a vault routine during the 2000 Summer Olympic Games in Sydney, Australia.

One for All

Most Olympic medals are won by individuals. Gold, silver, and bronze medals are awarded for first, second, and third place. A medal is given to the individual who receives the top score on a single apparatus. A medal is also awarded to an individual all-around champion. The all-around champion is the gymnast who performs best on more than one apparatus.

Teams can also take home a medal by earning the five best scores in events throughout the competition. The team with the highest total scores wins the team championship. It is great to be a part of a winning team!

The Magnificent Seven

July 24, 1996, was a hot summer night in Atlanta, Georgia. It looked like the Russian team would win the gold medal. Then a young American named Kerri Strugg hobbled into position on a bad ankle and launched her vault. Kerri inspired the rest of the U.S. team, and the Magnificent Seven—Amy Chow, Amy Borden, Dominique Dawes, Shannon Miller, Dominique Moceanu, Jaycie Phelps, and Kerri—took home the gold. It was the first team championship the U.S. women's gymnastics team had ever won!

Gymnastic Giants

There are many great athletes in gymnastics history. Here are two whom everyone remembers.

Olga Korbut

Olga Korbut was born on May 16, 1955, in Grodno, Belarus. She stood less than 5 feet (1.5 m) tall and weighed only 85 pounds (39 kilograms) when she walked into the Sporthalle in Munich, Germany, for the 1972 Summer Olympic Games. She left a huge impression that the world will never forget. Olga took home three Olympic gold medals in 1972 and was named "Athlete of the Year" by ABC's *Wide World of Sports*. In 1976, she won a fourth gold medal at the Montreal Olympics. In 1988, she was the first athlete inducted into the Gymnastics Hall of Fame. In 1994, she was named one of the top athletes in the past 40 years by *Sports Illustrated* magazine.

Kurt Thomas

Many consider Kurt Thomas the finest American male gymnast in history. He started competing in gymnastics during high school, and his small size allowed him to perform well. He weighed only 127 pounds (58 kg) by the time he was an adult. In 1978, Kurt Thomas won a gold medal in floor exercise at the World Gymnastics Championships in Strassbourg, Germany. He was the first American ever to win a gold at a world championship event. In 1979, he won two gold medals, the overall silver medal, and three other medals at the world championships. During his gymnastics career, Kurt won the U.S. National Championship three times. He won the Sullivan Award in 1979, which is given to the top amateur athlete in the United States. He is the only gymnast to win this award. In 2003, Kurt Thomas became a member of the International Gymnastics Hall of Fame.

What Happened When?

| 3000 B.C. | 393 | 1700 | 1800 | 1900 | 1930 | 1950 | 1970 |

3,000 B.C. Paintings, pottery, and other artifacts depict the first gymnasts. They are acrobats from ancient Egypt.

2,500 B.C. The first gymnastics apparatus is used in ancient Greece. It is a live bull.

776 B.C. The first Olympic Games are held in Athens, Greece. Only men are allowed to compete.

393 A.D. Roman Emperor Theodosius shuts down the Olympic Games.

1793 The first official gymnastics handbook, *Gymnastics for the Young*, by Johann Frederich Guts Muths, is published.

1811 Frederick Ludwig Jahn, the father of gymnastics, opens the first modern gymnasium near Berlin, Germany.

1881 The Fédération Internationale de Gymnastique is founded.

1896 The first modern Olympic Games are held in Athens, Greece, in a 2,000-year-old stadium.

1903 The first gymnastics world championships are held in Antwerp, Belgium.

1928 Women gymnasts compete for the first time in the Summer Olympic Games, but only in all-around team competitions.

1932 The United States takes home five gymnastics gold medals. This is its first big Olympic win in many years.

1952 Women compete in individual Olympic events for the first time ever.

1970 Cathy Rigby is the first American to win a medal at the World Championships.

Cathy Rigby

42

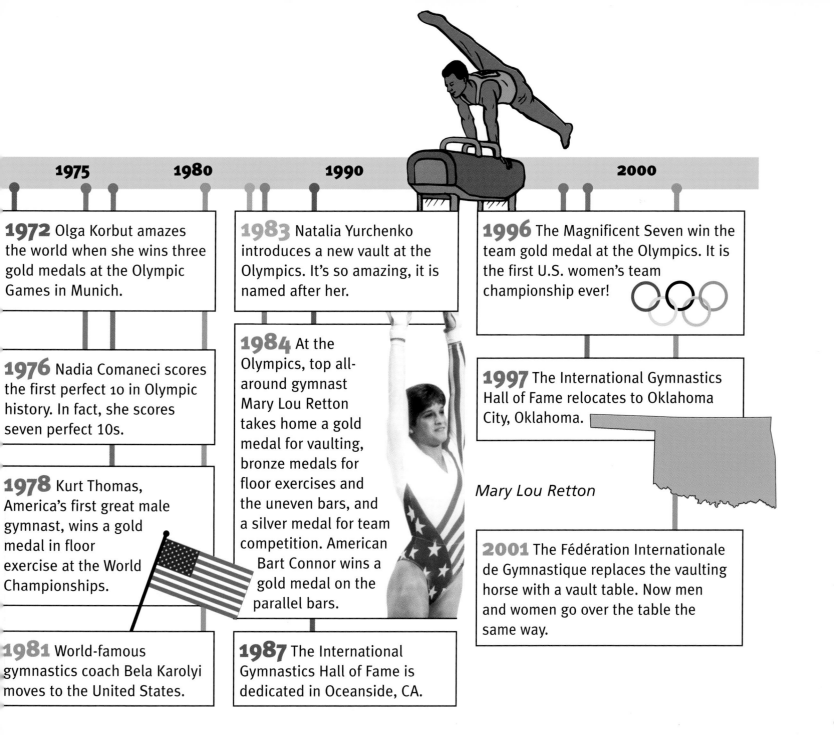

1975   **1980**   **1990**   **2000**

1972 Olga Korbut amazes the world when she wins three gold medals at the Olympic Games in Munich.

1983 Natalia Yurchenko introduces a new vault at the Olympics. It's so amazing, it is named after her.

1996 The Magnificent Seven win the team gold medal at the Olympics. It is the first U.S. women's team championship ever!

1976 Nadia Comaneci scores the first perfect 10 in Olympic history. In fact, she scores seven perfect 10s.

1984 At the Olympics, top all-around gymnast Mary Lou Retton takes home a gold medal for vaulting, bronze medals for floor exercises and the uneven bars, and a silver medal for team competition. American Bart Connor wins a gold medal on the parallel bars.

1997 The International Gymnastics Hall of Fame relocates to Oklahoma City, Oklahoma.

Mary Lou Retton

1978 Kurt Thomas, America's first great male gymnast, wins a gold medal in floor exercise at the World Championships.

2001 The Fédération Internationale de Gymnastique replaces the vaulting horse with a vault table. Now men and women go over the table the same way.

1981 World-famous gymnastics coach Bela Karolyi moves to the United States.

1987 The International Gymnastics Hall of Fame is dedicated in Oceanside, CA.

43

Gymnastics Gallery

The oldest gymnast to win an Olympic gold medal was Masao Takemoto of Japan. He won two silver medals and three bronze medals in 1952 and 1956. He was still on the team in 1960, when he was 40 years old.

Gymnastics has played a starring role on the big screen since the days of silent movies. Check out old-time movies like *The Thief of Baghdad* (1924) and today's *Spider-Man* (2002).

In 1896, the first modern-day Olympic Games were held in Athens, Greece. Nine sports were included. Gymnastics was one of them.

Sometime during the 770s B.C., a woman named Pherenice disguised herself as a man and won the Olympic cliff-diving competition. She was the first woman to compete in the Olympic Games!

Mitch Gaylord first thrilled the world in 1984, when he led the men's U.S. gymnastics team to its gold medal victory in the Olympics. In 1995, he was the stuntman for the role of Robin in the movie *Batman Forever*.

Early Olympic gymnastics events included fencing, wrestling, boxing, weight lifting, rope climbing, and club swinging. It took hundreds of years before gymnastics competitions included the events you see today.

In the late 1960s, the Andover, Massachusetts, gymnastics team included an athlete known as "Invincible Jay." Where is he today? On NBC late-night TV. His name is Jay Leno!

Gymnastics Words to Know

aerial: a move performed in the air

afterflight: a sequence of moves in which the gymnast lifts off the vault, using the hands for height

apparatus: a piece of equipment used in gymnastics events

artistic gymnastics: a form of gymnastics performed on apparatuses

balance beam: a long, narrow, wooden board used in gymnastics events

dismount: a move used to get off a piece of gymnastics equipment

Fédération Internationale de Gymnastique: the official governing organization for gymnastics competitions

flight element: a series of gymnastics moves performed in the air

floor: a carpeted area that sits on a soft platform, used for floor exercises in gymnastics events

gymnasium: the place where gymnasts practice

horizontal bar: a single rod that is elevated above the ground and used in gymnastics events

Iron Cross: a difficult feat performed on the rings, in which gymnasts hold their arms and legs perfectly straight while pushing out from the shoulders

L-support: a gymnastics move, performed on the rings or parallel bars, in which a gymnast extends both legs straight out from the waist so that the body resembles the letter "L"

landing: another word for dismount

parallel bars: a pair of wood or wood-coated fiberglass rods used in gymnastics events

planche: a gymnastics move performed on the rings, in which gymnasts suspend their bodies face down and parallel to the floor

pommel horse: a padded table covered with leather or suede with two U-shaped handles on top, which is used in gymnastics events

preflight: the step in a vault routine where gymnasts use their hands to lift off the vault and perform specific moves

progressions: a series of gymnastics moves performed in sequence

rhythmic gymnastics: a form of gymnastics performed on the floor with hand-held apparatuses

rings: a pair of wooden or fiberglass hoops used in gymnastics events

routine: a full exercise consisting of all the moves a gymnast uses

run-up: a standard approach used in vault routines

safety mat: a portable, cushioned surface placed below apparatuses to protect gymnasts if they fall

salto: somersaults or flips performed in the air

springboard: a flexible board mounted on springs that helps a gymnast gain momentum and height

vaulting horse: a padded table used in gymnastics events

Y-scale: a pose in which a gymnast brings one leg up to his or her head without bending it

Metric Conversion
1 yard = .9144 meters

Other Words to Know

Here are definitions for some of the words used in this book:

acrobatic: having to do with feats of agility and balance

agile: the ability to move in a quick and easy way

arena: an auditorium for sports events

balance: the art of holding the body in a single, difficult position

composition: an arrangement of gymnastics moves used in a routine

cushioned: padding added to an object, such as a floor or a chair, to make it soft

execution: the act of putting on a performance

fiberglass: a strong, flexible material made from glass fibers and resin

flexible: the ability to bend or move easily

freestanding: something that stands alone or without support

injury: damage to a part of the body, which can happen playing sports

originality: a fresh and unique style

pendulum: an object that swings back and forth freely

spectator: someone who observes an event

strength: having to do with physical power

torso: the upper part of the human body

Where To Learn More

AT THE LIBRARY

Gutman, Dan. *Gymnastics: The Trials, The Triumphs, The Truth*. New York: Puffin Books, 1996.

Jackman, Joan. *DK Superguides: Gymnastics*. United States: Dorling Kindersley Publishing, Inc., 1995.

Kalman, Bobbie and Crossingham, John. *Gymnastics in Action*. New York: Crabtree Publishing Company, 2003.

ON THE ROAD

Karolyi's World Gymnastics Summer Camps
454 FS 200
Huntsville, TX 77340
936/291-0007

International Gymnastics Hall of Fame
120 N. Robinson Avenue
Oklahoma City, OK 73102
405/235-5600
http://www.ighof.com

ON THE WEB

Fédération Internationale de Gymnastique
http://www.fig-gymnastics.com

USA Gymnastics
http://www.usa-gymnastics.org

INDEX

ABOUT THE AUTHOR

Beth Gruber has written about, edited, and reviewed children's books for almost 20 years. She has also interviewed authors and TV show creators who write for children. Beth lives in New York City and is excited to be writing her first children's book. She is a graduate of NYU School of Journalism. Reading and writing are her passions. Gymnastics is her favorite Olympics event.